WM. B. EERDMANS
PUBLISHING CO.
Grand Rapids, Michigan

MARSHALL PICKERING
CHRISTIAN since 1794 PUBLISHERS

MARY
An ordinary woman through whom God gave
the world his greatest gift
Retold by Marlee Alex
Illustrated by Ruth Imhoff, a Swiss artist
living in France.
© Copyright 1986 by Scandinavia
Publishing House, Nørregade 32, DK-1165 Copenhagen K.
English language edition first published 1987
through special arrangement with Scandinavia
jointly by W. B. Eerdmans Publishing Co.,
255 Jefferson Ave. S.E. Grand Rapids, Michigan 49503
and
Marshall Pickering, 3 Beggarwood Lane, Basingstoke,
Hants RG23 7LP, England
All rights reserved
Printed in Singapore
Eerdmans **ISBN 0-8028-5018-9**
Marshall **ISBN 0-551-014849**

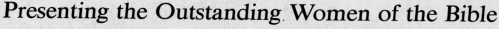

Presenting the Outstanding Women of the Bible

The Bible is the story of God's dealings with his people. This story is like a picture God painted for all the world to see. God wanted to show everyone, everywhere, how much he loves ordinary people, and how he can make wonderful things happen through ordinary lives.

Israel was a nation with laws and traditions which gave men the leadership in government and family life. However, Israel's history is full of stories of women. Some of these women rose to become leaders. Others shaped and changed the life of their nation as they stayed in the background. These stories stress the unique influence women can have on history.

In Israel, the influence of women might have been limited by the customs and laws of their country, or by personal things such as the amount of money they had, the type of education, their husband's position, or the number of children in the family. But in these stories we meet woman after woman who, in spite of outward hindrances, was limited only by the degree of her faith in God or by the degree of her determination to use the gifts he gave her.

We hope this book will make you eager to be used by God, and help you to believe more than ever before that you can be all God made you to be.

MARY

**An ordinary woman through whom God gave
the world his greatest gift**

Retold by Marlee Alex
Illustrated by Ruth Imhoff

William B. Eerdmans Publishing Company
Grand Rapids, Michigan

Marshall Pickering
Basingstoke, England

ello, Mary! God loves you," said a quiet voice.

Mary opened her sleepy eyes and looked up toward the open window. Light flooded her small bedchamber.

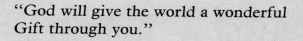

"God will give the world a wonderful Gift through you."

Mary heard, but could not see anyone. The light penetrating her room was brighter than the usual morning sun. It frightened her. But Mary admitted to herself, "It's not every day someone wakes me, saying something this exciting." So Mary waited and kept her eyes on the river of light.

As she watched, Mary realized it was a shining angel. It was the angel Gabriel. "Don't be afraid, Mary," Gabriel said. "God wants to show the world that He loves and cares for everyone. Your life is part of His plan."

Mary stared at the angel.

Gabriel continued, "God has chosen you to be the mother of His own Son. This time next year you will give birth to a baby boy. Name Him Jesus, because Jesus means 'savior.' Jesus will save people from the suffering and death caused by sin. He will teach people how to enter the kingdom of God, a kingdom that will never end."

Mary rose up off her bed. "But I am so young!" she exclaimed. "I am not even married yet. I have never lived with a man. How can I have a baby?"

"It will happen in a way that has never happened before, and will never happen again," Gabriel assured Mary. "The Baby will be conceived by the power of God's Holy Spirit. He will be the Son of God Himself.

"And by the way," Gabriel added, "did you know that Elizabeth and Zacharias, your mother's relatives, are also going to have a baby?"

"But Elizabeth is too old to become pregnant," Mary protested.

"Yet, it is true!" exclaimed Gabriel. "She is already pregnant. God makes things possible that no one would dare to imagine!"

Mary's face lit up with joy. "I am really just a girl, the most ordinary girl in Nazareth. But I have always loved God and longed to be used by Him. I will do whatever He says. I do hope what you are saying is true."

4

amazing thing that was supposed to happen to her, she dared not tell Joseph about it.

Several days passed. Then Mary packed some clothes and started out over the hills of Galilee towards Judea where Elizabeth, her mother's cousin, lived. Elizabeth was much older than Mary. As a little girl, Mary had often climbed up on her lap and listened to stories about the children of Israel and God's promise of a great king and savior. It was Elizabeth who had been the source of inspiration in Mary's life and who had taught her to love God. Although Mary was eager to talk to Elizabeth about this

Joseph was the man Mary would soon marry. The wedding festivities had been planned for months. Mary wondered as she skipped down the narrow roads of Galilee, "Will Joseph believe I talked to an angel? What will he think when he finds out I am going to have a baby? Will he understand that it is God's own Child?" The questions and worries flowed endlessly through Mary's mind as she hiked over the rocky hills of Judea. "Perhaps serving God is not going to be as simple as I dreamed it would," she thought to herself.

At last Mary climbed the stone steps leading to Elizabeth's house. "Hello!" she called out. "Is anyone home? Elizabeth, it's me, Mary!"

Elizabeth was just inside the door. At the sound of Mary's voice, she felt her own unborn baby leap in her womb. Elizabeth was filled with the Holy Spirit. She began to exclaim happily as she flew down the steps, "Mary! What a blessing you bring with you, for you have been chosen by God above all other women. And the Child you will bear will be God's greatest Gift to the world. Mary, what an honor to have you visit me. At the sound of your voice even my baby jumped for joy. For you believe God will do whatever He promises!"

Mary threw her arms around Elizabeth. "How can it be you know these things already?" she asked.

Mary's heart was filled with awe. "How happy I am in God, my Savior," she exclaimed. "How wonderful He is to look down and notice me. Surely, no one has ever known such joy. God has done great things for me! His love never ends; it is there for anyone who trusts Him."

Mary felt as if someone beyond herself were pouring these words of praise through her lips and saturating her heart with peace and joy. She lifted her hands toward the heavens and began to sing. "The arm of God is strong. He scatters all who think they are important. He takes power away from kings and princes, but gives success to those who are humble. He fills the empty-hearted, but empties the hearts of those who think they have everything. Just look how He has helped Israel! He has never forgotten to show them mercy. He promised He would always love them."

Mary stayed with Elizabeth for about three months. The two women shared God's promises, and prayed together about the future. They spun wool, dyed it, and wove pretty baby blankets. They talked endlessly about what it would be like to raise little boys. They laughed, thinking forward to the time when the two boys could romp and play together.

8

When Mary returned to Nazareth her womb began to grow round like Elizabeth's. Mary knew it would soon be obvious to her family and friends that she was expecting a baby. It was time to talk to Joseph about it.

Mary wandered slowly through the narrow streets of Nazareth to Joseph's carpenter shop. He would be working this time of day. As she stepped out of the sunny street into the cool shadow of the workshop, Mary felt hopeful Joseph would understand. "Joseph," she said softly, "do you remember that the prophet Isaiah promised a son born in Israel who would be called the Prince of Peace?"

Then Mary told Joseph the angel Gabriel had come to her saying she was to be the mother of this Prince, God's Son. She told about her visit with Elizabeth. "Elizabeth already knew about this Child before I told her anything. She confirmed the words of the angel," Mary explained.

Joseph looked skeptical and angry, but he didn't say anything for a long time. Finally he answered, "Mary, I love you and want to trust you. But your story is unbelievable. I know God has promised a savior to Israel. But how can you expect me to believe this savior will come through an ordinary young woman like you? Don't tell me lies, Mary. If you are going to have a baby, and I am not the baby's father, then we can never be married. I am disappointed and sorry, but I don't want to shame you. I will not tell anyone else about this. We'll break our engagement quietly."

Mary could not convince Joseph she was telling the truth. She left him alone and went home. "Joseph will never want to see me again," she thought sadly.

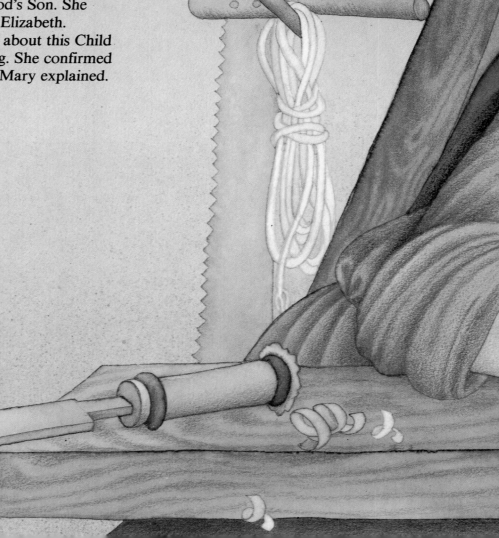

Day after day passed. Night after night Joseph lay awake, tossing and turning on his bed. He could not get Mary out of his mind. One night when he was half-asleep and half-awake he thought he dreamed someone was standing beside his bed. But Joseph wasn't dreaming. It was an angel.

The angel whispered, "Joseph, Joseph! Go ahead and make Mary your wife, for what she has told you is true. The child she carries in her womb is God's own Child, conceived by the Holy Spirit. It will be a baby boy. Name Him Jesus, for

He will save His people from their sin. He is the One God spoke of through His prophets, long ago."

Joseph could not sleep at all the rest of the night. The next morning he hurried down the hillside to the house where Mary lived. Taking her by surprise, he pleaded, "Forgive me, Mary. Last night an angel appeared to me in a dream and assured me everything you said was true. The angel said we should go ahead and be married while you wait for the birth of Jesus. I praise God for your faith, Mary."

So Joseph and Mary were married as planned. Mary began to make a cozy home for Joseph and the baby. Eventually, the time grew close for her baby to be born. Mary was nervous and excited. She wanted everything to be ready and just right. Then something happened to upset her plans.

The Roman Emperor, Caesar Augustus, decided to find out exactly how many people were under his authority. He wanted to brag about it to his friends. He ordered everyone in his empire to make a trip to the birthplace of their grandparents in order to be counted and classified.

"We'll have to go to Bethlehem," Joseph told Mary. "Bethlehem is the home town of my ancestor, King David. You are to be counted as a member of my family, Mary."

"But Bethlehem is so far away!" Mary exclaimed. "The baby is due to be born any day now. What if he is born along the way, so far from home?"

"The emperor has ordered it, Mary," Joseph sighed. "No one can be excused from the trip."

The way was long and the roads were very crowded, but at last Joseph and Mary reached Bethlehem, a small village surrounded by fields and meadows. It was the home of shepherds and farmers, people living a quiet life.

Mary was exhausted from the journey. She felt a twinge of pain as she sat down to rest in the shade. Joseph set out to look for a place to stay. "Don't worry, Mary. I'll find a nice, comfortable room and a warm, clean bed for you," he said.

Mary's womb was large and heavy now. Although the trip would be difficult, causing her and Joseph to travel slowly and carefully, they decided to trust God. "Perhaps this trip is part of God's plan," Mary pondered. "Surely, He will protect us and the baby."

When Joseph returned, he looked angry and upset. "Mary, there are no more rooms available at the village inn. I've looked everywhere possible. But the innkeeper said there is fresh hay in the stable. He agreed we could sleep there tonight, and tomorrow I'll look for a better place."

"Oh, Joseph," Mary cried. "I think the baby will be born tonight! We can't stay in a stable!"

"Mary, people are already bedding down under the trees," Joseph explained. "At least we can be alone if we stay in the stable. And the animals will keep it warm. We decided to trust God, remember? That means right now, even though it seems more difficult than ever."

Mary's face was contorted in disappointment and worry. The twinges of pain had given way to strong squeezing contractions in her womb. She knew she

had no choice but to let God have control over her feelings and her fears. It was just that everything seemed so wrong, so unlike she imagined it would be. She didn't even have a place to wash the baby or the clothes she'd brought along for Him. Besides, the streets of Bethlehem were full of Roman soldiers who did not even believe in the one true God.

Joseph helped Mary reach the stable. She lay down on the straw and gasped for breath as she labored to give birth to the Son of God. Late, late that very night, Joseph bent down over Mary's sweaty face and whispered, "Ten fingers! Ten toes! Oh, Mary, He is perfect."

Mary took her newborn in her arms and held Him close. "He is beautiful," she beamed. "Welcome, little Jesus. Welcome to our world. And thank you for coming." Mary wrapped the baby in clean swaddling clothes and laid Him to sleep in the fresh hay beside her. The only cry was the muffled bellow of a calf.

Joseph lay down beside Mary. "I feel like running out and telling everyone what happened here tonight," he said.

Mary pulled him close. "Joseph, God has His own way of sharing this good news. Let's wait and see whom he tells first."

Mary lay awake thinking about all that had happened since the angel Gabriel had appeared to her. She treasured the memories. As she looked at baby Jesus,

she thought she heard faint strains of music in the distance. It sounded like no earthly music she'd ever heard. "Joseph," she whispered, "do you hear music? It almost sounds like angels singing." But Joseph didn't answer. He was fast asleep.

As Mary drifted off to sleep, the chorus filled the cold night air: "Glory to God in the highest, and on earth, peace, goodwill to men."

Joseph and Mary stayed in Bethlehem until baby Jesus was sturdy enough to travel. On the way home they passed through the city of Jerusalem. There they stopped at the temple to dedicate Jesus to the Lord.

An old man named Simeon lived in Jerusalem. Simeon had been praying all his life for the savior God had promised. Simeon hoped to see this savior himself. In fact, God had once given him a promise that he would see the savior before he died.

When Mary and Joseph arrived at the temple with baby Jesus, Simeon was there, too. He hobbled back to Mary on his cane and gently lifted the baby from her arms. "You kept your promise, Lord!" Simeon said. He was so excited he almost shouted. "This boy is the Light that will shine upon all nations of the world and will be the King of Israel."

Mary did not know how to respond. She stood there in astonishment, marvelling at Simeon's words. Simeon turned to her and looked directly into her eyes. His expression was tender and loving.

"Mary," he said, "Your son will be hated by many people in this country. They will make Him suffer in a way that will make you very sad, so sad it will feel like a sword piercing your own heart. But many other people will believe in Jesus. They will know He is God's greatest Gift to the world! His love and joy will fill their lives. His life and death will be like keys to open secret places of the heart and make dreams come true."

As Mary listened to Simeon, she tried to imagine what was going to happen in the coming years. She imagined the time and energy she would pour into raising Jesus, the joy she would feel watching Him grow, the disappointment when people did not understand who He was. Mary imagined the sword that might one day be thrust into Jesus' side. She knew she would feel the pain in her own heart.

"Can I possibly bear all this?" she asked herself. "Am I willing to be a part of God's plan after all?"

Simeon returned baby Jesus to the arms of His mother. Mary's mind was racing. "Dear Lord," she prayed silently. "I am just beginning to understand what it means to serve You. I once thought it meant You would fill my life with miracles, that things would always go right. I was so eager to receive Your blessings. Now I'm beginning to see that the greatest blessings of life often come in ways we do not expect. Serving You will mean devoting myself to the ordinary things, like mothers do all day long, and being willing to trust You even when dreams seem to die. Lord God, You specialize in doing the impossible. Make these things possible in my life."

Holding her baby to her breast, Mary thought about the glorious things that lay behind her and the difficult things still ahead of her. The greatest miracle of all was happening in her own heart.